Lab
Retrievers

KV-683-403

Hamlyn **DOG BREED** Handbooks

Labrador & Golden
Retrievers

Angela Sayer & Edward Bunting

HAMLYN

First published in 1988
by The Hamlyn Publishing Group Limited,
a Division of The Octopus Publishing Group plc,
Michelin House, 81 Fulham Road,
London SW3 6RB.

ISBN 0 600 55792 8

Printed by Mandarin Offset in Hong Kong

Contents

Introduction

The sturdy, weatherproof character of the Labrador Retriever is a reflection of the harsh climate and rugged terrain of Newfoundland, where the breed has its origins. In its varied history it has worked as a sea fishermen's dog, retrieving cod that slipped the nets, and as a gundog on both sides of the Atlantic.

No Labrador Retriever in the UK today can attain the status of a full champion until it has received a working certificate as a gundog. But even those that live as pets, without any field training, show all the classic features of a gundog's nature – trainable, willing to work, keen on country walks and very good at playing 'fetch'.

These tough, unstoppable dogs have a 'soft' mouth – their teeth can grip without hurting – so they are also famous for their gentleness with children.

They are the all-rounders of the canine world – adept at fieldwork, showing, military service, police work and at drug-detecting for the customs service; and they are extremely reliable as guide dogs for the blind.

These combined abilities, and the unmistakable charm and 'personality' of the Labrador, have gained it immense popularity. In terms of all breed registrations with the Kennel Club, it took second place in 1986 with 14,625 puppies entered on the books. The second most popular of the 5 retriever breeds was the Golden Retriever with 11,948 registrations. (The other breeds in the retriever family – the Flatcoated, Curly-coated and Chesapeake Bay – amassed a joint total of approximately 1,000 registrations.)

The Labrador's worldwide popularity is evidenced by the fact that the Labrador Retriever Club has members in more than 26 countries besides Britain. British breeding stock has been used as the foundation of breeding kennels overseas, and British show and field

A Labrador sniffer dog works with unerring accuracy

trial judges are sought as experts wherever the qualities of the Labrador are recognized.

The Golden Retriever was bred in Scotland in Victorian times. Its ancestors include the now extinct Tweed Water Spaniel and the Irish Setter. The result is a strong, intelligent dog with a will to work and an air of understanding, as if it always knows just what its master is about to do next.

One of the things the breeders were aiming to do was to fix the glorious golden hue that was found in some retrievers, producing a breed that would always have it without fail. The coat can be either flat or wavy, with light, soft feathering; yet this is not a difficult dog to groom.

Always relaxed and confident, the Golden Retriever is one of the quietest and best behaved dogs in existence. It is extremely effective in the field, affectionate in the home and versatile as a working dog in modern society.

Overseas the Golden Retriever is well known too, with a huge following in Scandinavia and North America, and plenty of clubs in Australia and western Europe.

Breed standards

You may be so pleased with your retriever that you are considering taking it to a show. You want to know its chances: what do judges look for in your particular breed?

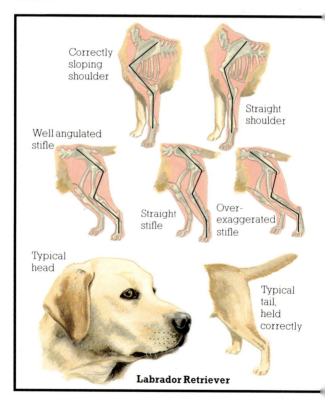

Correctly sloping shoulder

Straight shoulder

Well angulated stifle

Straight stifle

Over-exaggerated stifle

Typical head

Typical tail, held correctly

Labrador Retriever

For each breed that it recognizes, the Kennel Club draws up a list of features called a standard. This is worked out in agreement with the breed clubs.

Obviously the standard is a written document and as such can be interpreted in various ways – it is a matter of experience and individual preference.

Judges differ, for judging is an art; but it is found highly useful to have an official standard as a frame in which to measure the qualities of each individual dog, and these illustrations are based on the 'ideal' set out in the standard for the breed.

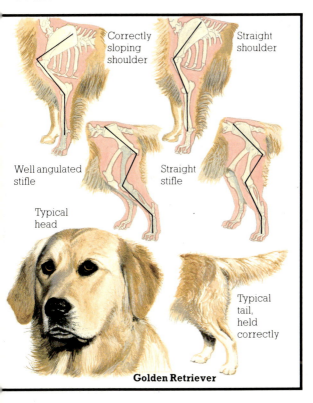

Correctly sloping shoulder

Straight shoulder

Well angulated stifle

Straight stifle

Typical head

Typical tail, held correctly

Golden Retriever

Labrador Retriever

Ears   Not too large or heavy, should hang close to head; set relatively far back on head

Eyes   Medium size, brown or hazel, expressing intelligence and good temper

Head   Broad skull with powerful jaws of good length and clearly visible 'stop' (stepdown in profile from forehead to muzzle)

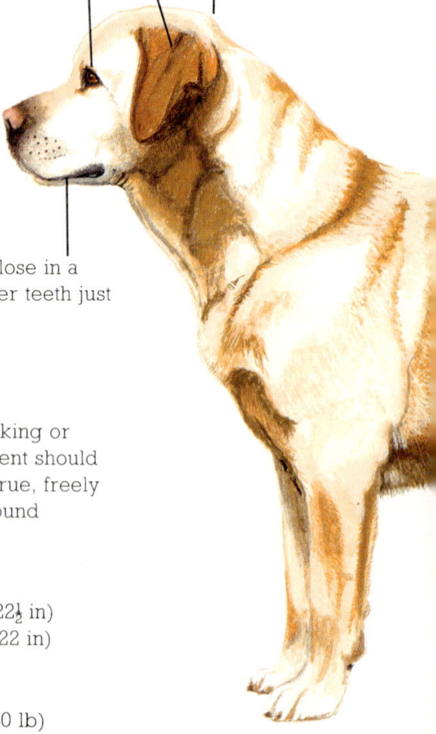

Mouth   Teeth close in a scissor bite (lower teeth just fit inside upper)

Gait   When walking or running, movement should be straight and true, freely covering the ground

Height
♂ 56–57 cm (22–22½ in)
♀ 54–56 cm (21½–22 in)

Weight
♂ 32–37 kg (70–80 lb)
♀ 27–32 kg (60–70 lb)

Body Deep, broad chest with barrel rib-cage; strong and well angulated shoulders and hindquarters; short back

Coat Dense, short and waterproof

Colours Solid, black or yellow or chocolate (rare); a white spot on the chest is acceptable

Tail Rounded, thick at base, tapering to tip (otter tail); may be carried gaily, but should not curl over the back

Golden Retriever

Ears Well proportioned, of moderate size, neatly set on to the head

Eyes Dark, well set, with dark rims; a kindly expression

Nose Should be black

Head Broad skull well set on a clean and muscular neck; muzzle wide and powerful

Mouth Teeth close in a scissor bite (lower teeth fit just inside upper)

Height
♂ 56–60 cm (22–24 in)
♀ 51–56 cm (20–22 in)

Weight
♂ 32–37 kg (70–80 lb)
♀ 27–32 kg (60–70 lb)

Body Well balanced, short coupled (ie spine is not too long); deep through the heart; ribs deep and well sprung

Coat Flat or wavy with a good feathering and dense, water-resistant undercoat

Colour Any shade of gold or cream but neither red nor mahogany; no more white than a few white hairs on chest

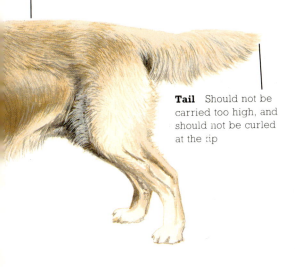

Tail Should not be carried too high, and should not be curled at the tip

Registering and showing

When pedigree puppies are born, it is normal to register them with the Kennel Club. It is best, and cheapest, if the breeder registers them, but you can do so if you have just bought a puppy and find it is not registered but have the necessary information. In any event, the litter itself has to be given an initial registration by the breeder.

The breeder fills in a Kennel Club registration form, which is dual-purpose: either it can be used for the initial registration of the litter, or it can be used to register each puppy, complete with names and colours.

Registration is crucially important if you ever want to take up showing or breeding for show, for any dogs that lack registration papers will never be able to attend any show of any importance, nor will their offspring.

Ownership is shown by a Kennel Club transfer form, which nowadays is on the reverse of the registration document.

A pedigree dog has a kennel name, given to it by the breeder, which normally consists of the affix and the dog's individual name. The affix is a name that identifies the dog as coming from the kennels at which it was born, and so has a function similar to our surnames. It can be either a prefix or a suffix.

Once a dog is registered, its kennel name cannot be changed (but if the new owner already has a registered affix, this may be added) and no other dog can be given the same name within less than 10 years.

The dog's everyday or 'calling' name may be different from the kennel name and is the name to which the dog responds and which is used to give commands.

Types of show

Exemption show For this, dogs are exempt from the need to be registered. It is the most informal, and is not held by a breed club: charities, agricultural shows and village fêtes are the usual sponsors.

Sanction show This is an informal members-only show held by a local canine society or breed club. For example, the Alnwick and District Canine Society holds a sanction show in February each year.

Limited show Also organized by a local society, but at a more formal level.

Open show Open to any dog that is registered; it is held by a local canine society or breed club. For example, the East Anglian Labrador Retriever Club holds its open show in November.

Championship show This is an open show of a more formal and advanced standard, where the Kennel Club offers Challenge Certificates for the best of sex. Clubs are allowed to hold three open shows a year, of which only one may be a championship. If a dog wins three Challenge Certificates under different judges and at different shows, it gains the title of Show Champion.

The biggest championship shows for retrievers are: (i) the Golden Retriever Club's Breed Championship Show, held in the first weekend of April at Stoneleigh near Kenilworth, Warwickshire, as part of the Royal Agricultural Show. In an average year there are some 600 dogs to look at.

(ii) The Labrador Retriever Club Championship Show, held at Towcester Racecourse in Northamptonshire in the first weekend in June. It has an average entry in the region of 400 Labradors.

In addition there are the group and general championship shows such as Cruft's and the regional ones held round the United Kingdom, such as the Birmingham Show. These are the really large affairs capturing the news media, but are of less concern to the owner who is just beginning as a breeder and show enthusiast.

Golden Retriever Clubs

The Golden Retriever Club Mrs T E Theed, Squirrelsmead Cottage, Fivehead, Taunton, Somerset. Tel: 0823 490445

Berkshire Downs and Chilterns Golden Retriever Club Mrs M Iles, Crofter's Heron, Fox Amport, Andover, Hampshire. Tel: 0264 88 616

Eastern Counties Golden Retriever Club Mrs Barbara Webb, Woodbarn, 116 Cambridge Road, Gt Shelford, Cambs. Tel: 0223 842358

Golden Retriever Club of Northumbria Mrs G Hudspith, Orana, Hawkewell, Stamfordham, Newcastle-upon-Tyne. Tel: Stamfordham 479

Golden Retriever Club of Scotland Mr E Fogg, 7 Pitcullen Terrace, Perth PH2 7EQ. Tel: 0738 24751

Golden Retriever Club of Wales Mr A Fall, 3 Curlew Close, Rest Bay, Porthcawl, Mid Glam. Tel: 065 6712742

Midland Golden Retriever Club Mr R A Hibbs, 8 Overdale Road, New Mills, Nr Stockport, Cheshire. Tel: Disley 2122

Northern Golden Retriever Association Mrs M Dawson, The Poplars, Donington, Northorp, Spalding, Lincs. Tel: Spalding 820278

North West Golden Retriever Club Mrs J Robinson, 32 Meadow Croft, Euxton, Nr Chorley, Lancs. Tel: 02572 62416

Southern Golden Retriever Society Mrs G Clark, Stocks Green Cottage, Rings Hill, Hilldenborough, Nr Tonbridge, Kent. Tel: 0732 838461

South Western Golden Retriever Club R Coward, Green Acres, Ibsley Drove, near Ringwood, Hants BH24 3NP. Tel: 0425 53146

Ulster Golden Retriever Club Mrs M Neill, 49 Brackagh Moss Road, Portadown, Co Armagh, Northern Ireland. Tel: 0762 840663

Cruft's, the world's most famous dog show

Labrador Retriever Clubs

The Labrador Retriever Club Mrs J Coulson,
Broadacre, Broad Lane, Hambledon, Hants.
Tel: 0701 32 385

East Anglian Labrador Retriever Club
Mrs L G Kinsella, The Mount, Fingringhoe,
near Colchester, Essex. Tel: 020 628 231

**Kent Surrey and Sussex Labrador Retriever
Club** Mrs L Newton, 59 Claygate Road, Dorking,
Surrey. Tel: Dorking 889384

Labrador Retriever Club of Northern Ireland
A J Kilpatrick Esq, 16 Corby Drive, Lisburn.
Tel: Lisburn 6573

Labrador Club of Scotland Mrs E W Nolan,
Veyatie Cottage, Kingswell Bridge, near Fenwick,
Ayrshire. Tel: Fenwick 332

Labrador Retriever Club of Wales
Mr G Howells, 18 Gwernant, Cwmllynfell, Swansea,
Glam. Tel: 063 978 403
Midland Counties Labrador Retriever Club
Mr F Whitbread, Blackbrook Farm, Mercaston Lane,
Nr Turnditch, Derbyshire DE5 2LU
**Northumberland and Durham Labrador
Retriever Club** Miss E Smith, 29 High Street,
Gosforth, Newcastle-upon-Tyne 3. Tel: 091 2852192
Northwest Labrador Retriever Club
Mrs E Grenhaigh, Bank House, Bold Lane, Collins
Green, Warrington, Cheshire. Tel: 092 52 6778
Three Ridings Labrador Club Mrs P M Gill,
Crossgreen Labradors, 77 Crossgreen, Otley,
West Yorkshire
West of England Labrador Retriever Club
Mrs N Leah, Old Orchard, Bounders Lane, Bolingey,
Perranporth, Cornwall TR6 0AS. Tel: 087 257 3192
Yellow Labrador Club Mr H W Clayton,
Ardmargha Cottage, Brighthampton, Standlake,
Witney, Oxon. Tel: 086 731 374

Other useful addresses

National Gundog Association Mrs A Webster,
The White House, Breedon, Brand, Osgathorpe,
Loughborough, Leicestershire LE12 9ST.
Gundog Breeds Association of Scotland
Mr F R Ellison, 2 North Kirklands, Eaglesham,
Glasgow G76 0NT.
The Kennel Club 1–5 Clarges Street, Piccadilly,
London W1Y 8AB
**Royal Society for the Prevention of Cruelty to
Animals (RSPCA)** The Causeway, Horsham,
West Sussex RH12 1HQ.
Our Dogs magazine, 5 Oxford Road, Station Approach,
Manchester M60 1SX.
Dog World magazine, 9 Tufton Street, Ashford,
Kent TN23 1QN.

Choosing the right puppy

When you are dealing with domestic animals, there are few sights as picturesque and lovable as a litter of young retrievers. They are *all* irresistible, so it is easy to be tempted and buy solely on impulse. Before you go shopping for your Golden or Labrador Retriever, it is wise to establish a set of firm rules: follow these, and you should prevent things from going wrong.

Begin by contacting a reputable breeder through the secretary of a club specializing in the retriever breed of your choice. Make an appointment to view the breeder's litter. When the time comes, do not be bullied into taking along family and friends: children in particular are easily captivated by the smallest or funniest puppy of the litter, which may also be the weakest and most delicate.

Points to look for in a new Retriever

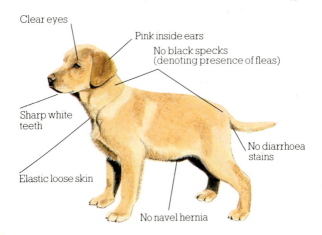

Clear eyes

Pink inside ears

No black specks
(denoting presence of fleas)

Sharp white teeth

No diarrhoea stains

Elastic loose skin

No navel hernia

A Golden Retriever mother with pups approaching weaning age

Judging the puppy

Ask to see the bitch, and also the sire of the litter if at all possible: in this way you will be able to form an opinion of the family tendencies in temperament, size and conformation. Ask to see the whole litter: they should *all* be in good condition.

Buy only from a breeder whose dogs are certified by the British Veterinary Association (BVA) as free from the known hereditary diseases (hip dysplasia and eye defects). It should be possible to buy a puppy whose parents and grandparents (at least) are certified free. The greater the depth of freedom from diseases in the pedigree, the better are your chances of having a puppy which will not develop these problems as an adult.

As a guideline look for hip results 'pass' or 'breeder's letter' or a low score (zero is perfect). Any pedigree which shows a number of unexamined ancestors or a number with high scores should be avoided.

Look at the breed standard ahead of your appointment, and when you have read it and think you know it, read it again: look, too, at pictures of excellent Golden and Labrador Retrievers, until you think you know a bit about what makes them such outstanding dogs.

Then decide which puppy in the litter is closest to the standard. At this point, if you are definitely not interested in showing or in fieldwork, you should still look for a happy, outgoing temperament.

If you wish to have a potential show dog, take the breeder's advice; a good breeder will ensure that you get a top quality puppy if you make it clear that you wish to show it. Having said that, no-one can ever guarantee that any puppy of 8 weeks will turn out to be a top winner. Breeders themselves usually keep potentially good puppies for up to 1 year before deciding which will make the top grade.

The young retriever should be cute, alert and interested. Although it is only a puppy, the basic proportions of skull and body should look right, and teeth should form a scissor bite, the upper front teeth closing slightly over the lower ones. The colour of Golden Retriever pups will be lighter than standard: look at the ears, for these will be close to the overall coat colour of the dog when fully grown.

Listen carefully to what the breeder tells you: most will give sound advice on correct rearing and care, and usually on making your choice out of the litter, too. And make sure that it's understood exactly what the agreed price will pay for. Does it include the papers, all signed and handed over on the spot? If you are going to show and breed, you must insist on receiving the registration document, as well as the pedigree.

Care of
the new puppy

You have chosen your young retriever: now it is time to fix a convenient date on which to collect it. Give yourself time to purchase all the necessary equipment and food: and arrange your diary dates so as to allow lots of time to be present in the home to settle the newcomer in.

Feeding

The question of feeding will be uppermost in your mind but it is unwise to print a feeding table in a book of this kind, for this would give the impression that anything else you are told is 'wrong'. What counts for more is what your puppy is used to. Ask for a diet sheet from the breeder to ensure continuity of feeding for at least the first few weeks – a change of diet will upset the puppy's stomach.

Safe environment

A young puppy will chew everything in easy reach, so reposition electric wires, anything that is made of loose man-made fibres such as a bed-spread or vulnerable doormat, and place small objects out of reach where they cannot be swallowed. If you can provide a mesh puppy-pen, or partition an area of the room with a baby's play-pen, or large wire fireguard, so much the better. The floor area should be washable, and you may wish to spread newspaper for the first few days.

Collect your puppy by car if possible. This avoids the risk of picking up diseases from another animal – even the ground is a source of infection.

Bear in mind that this journey is probably the most frightening experience that the animal will undergo in

Prepare a play-pen in advance

all its life. It is leaving its mother and siblings and being subjected to a range of unfamiliar scents, sights and sounds.

Car sickness is common in young puppies, so take lots of newspapers and an old towel to line the car and put on your lap. Morning is the best time for collecting a new puppy.

A selection of feeding bowls

Settling down

Get home as smoothly and quickly as possible, talking soothingly to the puppy, and offer a small feed of cereal and milk on arrival. After feeding, place the puppy on its toilet area (see page 29) then put it in its box with a soft blanket, and encourage it to sleep. If it whimpers or cries, comfort it and then settle it firmly back in the box.

At this stage the puppy's play periods are about 30 minutes long and are interspersed with long periods of sleep. At night the puppy will probably whimper and whine: offer a well-wrapped stone hot water bottle, or have an infra-red heater suspended over the box for added warmth and comfort.

Puppies and children

Healthy puppies enjoy playing with (kind) children. Teach the children how to groom the puppy; how to carry it correctly, with both arms encompassing the fore

The correct way to carry a puppy

Puppies sleep a great deal, with play periods of about 30 minutes

and hind legs; how to lift and put down the little dog; and how to help prepare its regular meals.

There are a few basic rules to protect both parties:

- Children must be taught to wash their hands after play sessions with the puppy.
- The puppy needs short sessions of deep sleep after each play session, and children must be taught to respect this. A puppy must never be allowed to become exhausted or overexcited.
- The puppy must not be allowed to play with items small enough for it to swallow or to get stuck in its throat.
- Do not pull it around on a lead or treat like a toy.

Exercise

A puppy up to 5 months of age requires no formal exercise, just play in the house and garden. From 5 months begin a little lead training, just a few yards at first. When the dog is 10 or 12 months of age it can begin to have more exercise and by 18 months should be having a good walk of 2/3 miles per day or preferably 1 hour free running if you have a convenient park or open ground. Too much exercise whilst a growing puppy puts undue strain on growing bones and joint formation.

Vaccination programme

Approximate age (take the vet's advice)	**Vaccination**
6–9 weeks	First canine distemper First canine hepatitis } combined First canine parvovirus First combined leptospirosis
About 12 weeks	Second canine distemper Second canine hepatitis } combined Second canine parvovirus Second combined leptospirosis First rabies (necessary if the dog lives in or will travel to countries where there is rabies; not normally given if dog is not leaving the UK)
14–16 weeks	Second rabies (if applicable)
16–20 weeks	Third canine parvovirus if applicable (depends on circumstances)
Annually	Canine distemper booster Canine hepatitis booster } combined Canine parvovirus booster Leptospirosis booster

Training

Retrievers are alert, intelligent dogs and they are easy to train if you are methodical and follow a few simple rules. But although gifted, they are still no more nor less than dogs, and so it is always necessary to keep your patience. Compared to your understanding, theirs is, after all, only a limited one.

House training

With some puppies, house training proceeds without any hitches, while with others it can seem a never-ending affair. It is one of the most important sets of lessons that a puppy has to learn and it must be given maximum patience.

Puppies must learn where they are, and are not, allowed to go

Whenever the puppy performs in an acceptable manner it must be warmly praised, but do not punish it when it makes a mistake: merely show it that such behaviour is not pleasing.

A careful watch on your puppy's habits will show you that it follows a natural pattern of activity:

1 Wakes from deep sleep.
2 Plays for 5–10 minutes.
3 Circles to and fro before defecating.
4 Plays for 15–20 minutes.
5 Sleeps deeply for about an hour.

This cycle is repeated throughout the day. Defecation also occurs about 5 minutes after each meal. The best method is to designate a special area outside as the dog's toilet area and at each of the predictable times the puppy is placed there. This practice will last the dog's lifetime if properly established.

House manners

The puppy must know where in the house it is allowed to go, and which areas are forbidden. It must learn which rooms it is allowed to sleep in, and whether armchairs are within its territory or not.

Placing the puppy on its patch

A training session: Golden Retrievers love every minute of it

Lead, collar and disc. Outside the home, dogs must wear identification

In this matter, it is absolutely vital to stick to what you have decided and never waver from enforcing it vigorously. Any time your word of command is ignored with impunity serves to encourage your puppy into further disobedience.

It is useful to teach the puppy to go into its bed or basket at a word of command, or even a hand signal. This should never be thought of as a punishment, and can be accompanied with a reward.

The collar and lead

At first the puppy will not need to be walked on the lead, for it will get sufficient exercise romping and playing at home. However, it is sensible to begin lead training at an early age.

During the first week of lead training, clip a light lead to the puppy's collar and leave it to trail on the ground for short periods. Follow this with some more serious training: hold the lead and encourage the puppy to walk with you, on your left.

Never use the lead as a means of pulling the puppy along, nor to smack it. Praise the puppy whenever it walks freely forward. The lead will become an object of pleasure to the dog, make sure it never becomes an instrument of punishment.

Basic obedience training

The very best way to learn to train your dog beyond this stage is to enrol in a dog-training class. These cater for all standards from the basics to competitive obedience work and besides giving you thousands of ideas, they provide a chance for the dog to socialize too.

Preliminary classes cover the basic commands, walking at heel and coming to call, while those who wish to progress to showing may attend ringcraft lessons.

Removing an object from the dog's mouth

Basic training is essentially about teaching your puppy to be considerate and obedient, to come *immediately* when called and to have acceptable manners in the home. Play is an important aspect in teaching manners, and it is vital that your dog really loves and respects you, so that you become its 'pack leader'.

Serious training should begin when your puppy reaches 6–8 months. You will need to buy a good quality check collar of the correct size for a retriever at this age. When this is put on at the start of each lesson, the puppy understands that it is time for work.

Training for the field

If you want your retriever to work as a gundog, this will call for specialist training from an early age. All dogs will learn to fetch objects thrown for them, and in retrievers the instinct is so well developed that there are stories of dogs that retrieve game naturally, without training. In practice, gundogs are 'forced' which is the term for systematic training that ensures the dog will know exactly what it has to do, will run exactly where it is directed and will release the game from its mouth without quibble.

From an early age your retriever will pick things up and carry them about. You can encourage the dog to bring them to you, take the object gently from its mouth, saying 'Dead' as you take it, praise the dog, and give it back.

If the object is something you don't want it to have, then give something else for the dog to carry instead. The key is to take it gently; do not snatch, or it may make him hard-mouthed. If you have to, pull the jaws apart, praising.

Two things are apparent from this: (i) that you have to have a good, trusting relationship with the dog; and (ii) children, who often love to play 'tug-of-war' with a puppy, must be strictly forbidden from doing so with a retriever destined for work in the field.

Retriever trials: dogs enjoy the chance to show their ability in the field

General care

If you can guarantee to provide enough exercise and good living conditions and love, this is the basic formula for the general care of the dog.

The Labrador has a short, dense coat

Bathing

Golden Retrievers: With regular grooming, a Golden Retriever doesn't need bathing very often. Most of them love to go swimming in rivers or lakes, and if yours is an outdoor dog and swims often, it will hardly ever have to have a bath. If it spends a lot of its time in centrally-heated rooms it may shed lots of hair, and this makes frequent baths a good idea. Besides taking out loose hairs it keeps the skin in good condition.

1 Carefully groom the coat from head to tail.
2 Place the dog in the bath and wash the face, using clean warm water.
3 Clean the eyes, nostrils and mouth.
4 Wipe out the ears with moistened swabs.
5 Carefully wet the ear flaps and work in a little shampoo to the edges to remove soil; rinse and dry with a towel.
6 Thoroughly wet the entire coat.
7 Apply a suitable shampoo, working it in well. Make sure no water or shampoo gets into the dog's eyes or ears.
8 Rinse every trace of shampoo from the coat with tepid water. Again, make sure no water goes into the eyes or ears.
9 Dry the dog thoroughly, using a rough towel, without delay.
10 Unless the dog objects, finish off the coat with a hair drier set to 'cool'. Carefully groom the coat into place while drying.

Labradors: A Labrador should not need bathing; regular brushing with a stiff bristle brush will keep the coat clean. If the dog gets really soiled, bath with a specially mild dog shampoo and dry thoroughly with rough towels, paying particular attention to the area of the rump and tail. Always bath early in the day to ensure the dog doesn't go to bed damp.

A selection of grooming equipment

Ears

The dog's ears should be examined at regular intervals and cleaned of any dark wax, though you must never probe inside the ear canal. A heavy build-up of waxy or greasy substances ('exudates') inside the ear flaps probably indicates the presence of ear mites, which are very annoying and will need a vet's prescription.

In the normal way, the ears are best wiped with cotton wool swabs. Dry swabs usually lift out the dirt and wax, but you can use damp swabs for resistant grime. Never allow water to get inside the ear.

Eyes

If the dog has been out in high grass or undergrowth, check for, and wash out, any foreign bodies or seeds. Water or a very weak solution of boric acid will be fine for cleaning the eyes.

Some dogs are prone to inflammation of the eyes due to a minor bacterial infection. To bathe the eyes, dip a cotton wool swab in saline solution and wipe from the outer corner to the inner one, then discard the swab and repeat with a fresh one. Treat each eye separately. Never use the same swab on both eyes.

For persistent eye trouble, a veterinary examination and prescription will be needed.

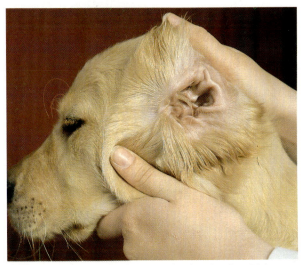

The weekly ear examination: the inside should be pink and clean

Teeth

The first teeth start to appear when the puppy is 3 weeks old and are generally all grown by 6 weeks. These are the milk teeth – they fall out from about 12 weeks to 16 weeks, when the permanent teeth grow.

This period when new teeth are 'erupting' beneath and between the milk teeth is one when special care is needed, as teeth will be crowded in the mouth and food particles can very easily get trapped and retained for a long time, leading to dental disease.

Clean the dog's teeth by rubbing them with a slice of lemon at regular intervals. (Some dogs resist tooth-brushing with determination, however.) If you prefer it, give the dog a small toothbrush and brush its teeth, using vinegar and water or salt water, or even toothpaste.

If tartar (a hard deposit) appears on the teeth (despite a good diet with hard biscuit), the vet will scale it.

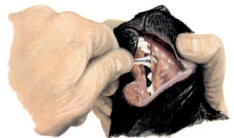

Tartar on the teeth

Nails and paws

A dog regularly exercised on hard surfaces keeps its nails at the correct natural length. Retrievers that go for long runs in fields and tracks may do the same, but those that live indoors or are confined to grass will have to have their nails trimmed.

The vet is the best person to instruct you in the use of special guillotine-type nail clippers to shorten your dog's nails, and to ensure that you know just where the quick (sensitive area) extends.

Clipping claws must be carried out with great care, avoiding the sensitive quick.

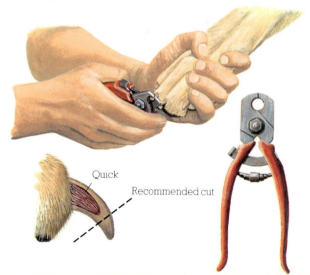

Quick

Recommended cut

Breeding

If you decide on breeding, you have one advantage already, for retrievers are probably the easiest of all dog breeds in giving birth.

The prime focus of your planning is the oestrous period. (This word is spelt 'oestrous' as an adjective and 'oestrus' as a noun.) It is the bitch's sexually receptive

Normal bitch mating cycle

Playful with dogs

Will accept stud during this period

Discharge bright red, turning pink, then cream coloured

Follicles developing toward surface of ovaries

1 2 3 4 5 6 7 8 9 10 11 12 13 14 15 16 17 18 19 20

Vulva swells
Appetite increases
Restlessness

Reproductive system becoming congested

Ovulation period

Ova moving down tubes

Will not accept stud

Remainder of half year ... 158 days

The oestrous cycle

time, when she will mate and conceive puppies. Most bitches come into season for the first time at about 8 months of age, though this varies with the individual; if a bitch has shown no sign of oestrus even at 15 months, consult a vet.

In all breeds, oestrus recurs at intervals of between 4 and 8 months, commonly 6 months, until late in the bitch's life.

Before contemplating breeding from a bitch (or using a dog at stud) ensure that both have been examined under the BVA schemes for hereditary defects (hips and eyes). Only dogs which reach an acceptable standard of freedom from these diseases should be used for breeding.

Signs of oestrus

Physical signs	Behavioural signs	Time span
Vulva enlarges and swells	Bitch may become irritable or extra sensitive	—
Bloodstained discharge appears (this is known as 'showing colour')	Bitch frequently cleans her genital area and may urinate more frequently than usual. Though attractive to male dogs the bitch will not 'stand' for mating.	Day 1–10
Red discharge ceases. Straw-coloured fluid appears.	Bitch should stand for mating.	*Day 10–18

*These dates are only guidelines: bitches may vary by several days. The best advice is to arrange to go to the dog on the 13th day of the season. This should not be too late, and if it is too early, you can return until you are successful.

Planning the family

It is not considered wise to mate a bitch during her first season, or even at the second oestrus if she is particularly juvenile in her attitude to life as she might not take a litter of puppies seriously enough. She should be at least 18 months old when she whelps.

Do not give contraceptive pills to a bitch that is destined for breeding, as these could interfere with the breeding pattern later in life. Just confine her indoors during her first season, protect her from the unwanted attention of male dogs, and wait for the following oestrous period to come round.

Long before this event occurs, you will have laid plans for the mating with a stud of your choice (again, see that the dog has a low hip score (page 23) and an up to date eye certificate). The bitch must be at the peak of health and strength when mating takes place, so build her condition up in the weeks prior to the event. Make sure she is completely free from parasites of any kind, and that any necessary annual booster doses in her vaccination programme have been carried out. See that she is on a diet that suits her digestion perfectly.

Again, long before mating you should arrange to have the bitch's hips X-rayed and scored for hip dysplasia. You should have her eyes examined for cataract and PRA under the BVA/Kennel Club Scheme. This must be done annually for all breeding stock.

Meanwhile you will have contacted the owner of your chosen stud and made the arrangements for a visit.

Going to stud

Mating may vary from a brief encounter to a protracted affair lasting over an hour. If the bitch is at the right stage in her season she should stand quietly while the dog mounts her and mating occurs.

Although one mating is generally sufficient, some breeders prefer to follow up with a second service within 48 hours.

How long to wait for the pups? It is usual to calculate 63 days from the first mating, as in the tables commonly printed in dog books. However, fertilization sometimes does not happen until some days afterwards, and this is a cause of 'late' litters.

It is always advisable to ensure that the business aspect of the visit is completed before you leave: pay the fee, and see that you get a certificate recording the mating and the pedigree of the stud. Keep this, as you will need it for registering the puppies.

Pregnancy

After the bitch is successfully mated, the fertilized egg takes about 10 days to travel to the uterus and another 10 days to become firmly attached to the uterine wall. At this stage the foetus is only 6–38 mm ($\frac{1}{4}$–$1\frac{1}{2}$ in) across and the bitch should be treated as normal, with no increase or change in her diet or exercise routine.

At 24–30 days' gestation a vet may be able to confirm the pregnancy by gentle palpation (feeling) of the bitch's abdomen. If for some special reason it is essential to have a diagnosis done by X-ray, this may be carried out in the last weeks of the pregnancy, when sufficient calcium has been laid down in the puppies' skeletons for them to resist the harmful effects of the radiation.

Phantom pregnancy

Whether a bitch is mated or not during her oestrus, the hormonal changes which naturally occur may cause a false or 'phantom' pregnancy. A bitch so affected goes through all the physical transformation seen in a true pregnancy and she may even make a whelping bed and appear to suffer birth pains. She will then adopt toys or other inanimate objects as substitute puppies.

Whelping

In the last week of pregnancy the whelping box is provided in place of the bitch's normal bed. If the

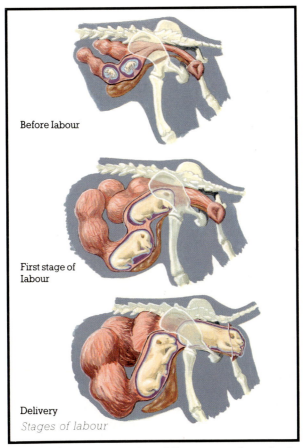

Before labour

First stage of labour

Delivery

Stages of labour

whelping is to take place in a different room from that in which she normally sleeps, be sure to move her at least a week before the due date.

You must be able to heat the whelping room (or area) if the need arises. Either heat the whole room or suspend a heat lamp over the whelping box. Newborn pups can sometimes become separated from their mother, lose body heat, then develop hypothermia and die unless you have supplementary heating.

Essential equipment

- Lots of clean newspaper for bedding.
- A bowl of water, soap and a towel for hand washing.
- A pair of sterilized stainless steel scissors.
- Some clean towels for drying the puppies.
- Plastic sack for soiled bedding and towels.
- A large box with hot water bottle and blanket, in which to keep the puppies if things go wrong.
- Scales, notebook and pencil for recording each birth.

Labour Behavioural changes in the bitch indicate the first stage – the onset of whelping. She is likely to refuse all food for 12–24 hours prior to the birth and may become very restless. She will probably be looking anxious, and panting.

She should not be left alone in the house, as her nest-making instincts will induce her to tear at anything, including soft furnishings as well as the bedding in her box.

A suitable whelping box

Care during pregnancy

Weeks after mating	Action
1 week	Start giving extra vitamins (Stress, or other calcium additive).
5 weeks	Give 2 small meals instead of one.
7 weeks	Increase meat gradually to 1 kg (2 lb) per day by whelping time. Also give milk and raw eggs.
7–8 weeks	Now divide the bitch's food into three well-spaced meals, giving a total volume of about $1\frac{1}{2}$ times normal. The food should be of the best quality and she may have milk to drink in addition to her normal fresh water. Do not overdo the mineral and vitamin supplements, but ensure with the vet that any actual deficiencies that she may suffer from are balanced. Prevent any sign of obesity by continuing sensible periods of exercise, but discourage strenuous running or jumping.
9 weeks	Treat the bitch with all consideration during this final stage of gestation. Feed her little and often, allow her to exercise as she pleases and ensure that she is able to relieve herself as often as she wishes.

The birth The straining of the bitch produces the first
water bag. This looks like a black or grey balloon, and
she generally ruptures it by biting or licking; this
releases a gush of greenish-black amniotic fluid. The
first puppy should follow quickly, born encased in a
membrane which the bitch licks away. Her licking
stimulates the puppy's first breath. If she neglects this
duty, you must remove the membrane, otherwise the
puppy will suffocate the moment the oxygen supply

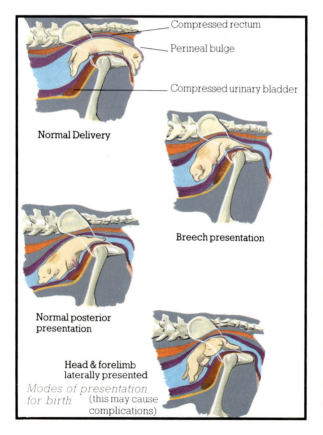

Compressed rectum

Perineal bulge

Compressed urinary bladder

Normal Delivery

Breech presentation

Normal posterior
presentation

Head & forelimb
laterally presented

*Modes of presentation
for birth* (this may cause
complications)

from the placenta is cut off. Clear the puppy's mouth and nostrils of mucus to allow a clear passage of air.

The third stage, which is the expulsion of the placenta, usually occurs about 15 minutes after that of the puppy. The bitch eats the placenta and bites through the umbilical cord. She then cleans up the birth fluids, licks the puppy and her own vulva, and settles down before the next puppy presents itself for birth.

Puppies may be born at regular intervals or they may come in batches or pairs with long intervals of rest ($\frac{1}{2}$–2 hours) in between. Retriever litters of both Golden and Labrador breeds average 7 or 8 in number, varying enormously from 1 to 12 in extreme cases, with the normal range between 6 and 10.

It is better to leave the bitch alone during whelping, but stay near her, helping only if she neglects her duties, or the puppies come so quickly that she cannot attend to them all. The owner's role should be passive, observant and comforting, but ready to call the vet if necessary.

How to help the newborn puppy

1 Break the membrane over the puppy's nose with your thumb-nail, then open its mouth and clear the mucus away with a paper towel.

The mother normally licks away the birth membrane

Reviving an apparently lifeless pup by draining the blocked breathing passages

2 Hold the puppy head down to allow fluid to drain, and if it appears lifeless, swing it gently to induce breathing.

3 When the puppy cries you may sever the cord with sterilized stainless steel scissors, leaving at least 2.5 cm (1 in) still attached to the pup.

4 Rub the puppy quite vigorously with terry towelling until it is dry and warm, and introduce it to the mother's teat.

All's well here – as it usually is

Problem births

Puppies may be born either head first or tail first, and there is no need to be alarmed if the hind feet are presented instead of the head. Most pups, once they start to emerge, are delivered within a few minutes, though the firstborn of any litter can present problems.

If a bitch strains for more than an hour without producing a puppy, or a puppy is halfway out and the bitch cannot complete the expulsion, the vet must be called.

- A bitch may develop 'uterine inertia' in which the womb seems too weak to contract sufficiently to expel the puppies. A vet can try to right this by means of injections: or it may be necessary to act surgically.
- A young or inexperienced bitch may seem afraid of her first puppy and seem reluctant to accept it. Lift this one from the whelping box, clean and dry it and place it in the special emergency box you have already prepared, where it can lie on a well-wrapped hot water bottle until the next puppy is born. Eventually the maternal instinct overcomes the bitch's initial fears and all the puppies are accepted.

Orphan or rejected puppies

If a bitch dies during whelping or has inadequate milk for the litter it may be necessary to hand rear puppies. This should never be undertaken lightly, for it is a demanding and very time-consuming job which has to be seen through to its conclusion.

Orphan puppies must be carefully fed, and kept clean and warm. They are best confined in an insulated box kept at a constant 30°C (86°F) for the first week of life, then at a temperature of 24–27°C (75–80°F) until weaning.

Feeding orphan puppies

It is best to use one of the commercially produced feeds, manufactured to simulate bitch's milk. Take every care

Feeding an orphaned puppy

with mixing this feed, and always ensure that all equipment is scrupulously clean.

Feed the puppies either from bottles specially designed for this purpose (available from suppliers of canine products) or from bottles that are manufactured for premature human babies. If the latter, fit teats that have enlarged holes.

During the first week, puppies should be fed on demand: this normally means every 2 hours during the day, with two or three feeds during the night.

- Tilt the bottle to prevent the puppies sucking air.
- The holes in the teat should be cut to allow a steady supply of milk, without inducing choking.
- After three weeks, introduce solid foods, while continuing milk feeds.

Simulating mother

Defecation and urination are normally stimulated during the puppy's first days of life by the bitch licking the anus, genitalia and abdomen. The orphan puppy is unable to pass faeces or urine unless it has this stimulus, so a warm wet piece of cotton wool must be rubbed gently over these parts until elimination has taken place.

Retriever puppies

Soon after birth, puppies move towards the warmth of their mother's body, seek out a teat and begin to suckle. The bitch is very protective during the first day or two and may be reluctant to leave her litter even to pass urine or to eat. As the weeks pass, her enthusiasm gradually diminishes, until six weeks after the birth she will want to spend only the briefest of periods with her offspring.

First three weeks During the first 10 days, puppies have their eyes tightly closed and they do little but feed, eliminate and sleep. Clip the nails weekly, mainly to prevent puppies with long claws from damaging the bitch's teats as they scrabble for milk. The dew claws (the dog's 'thumbs') need not be removed.

Navels should be checked daily – the dried cords drop off after two or three days – and any sign of inflammation or swelling must be reported to the vet immediately.

Puppies scrabble for their milk

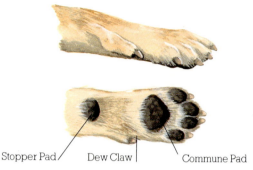

Stopper Pad /   Dew Claw | Commune Pad

Dew claws are no trouble to the dog if they are regularly clipped

Although their hearing is not very developed at this stage, you should talk to the puppies at all times to accustom them to the human voice.

Once their eyes are open, the puppies begin to exhibit the first play behaviour, and they start to lift their bodies up on to their legs rather than squirming around in their box.

The first teeth come at 14–21 days, and are needle-sharp.

From 3 to 6 weeks At 20 days the puppies can see and hear and are well up on their feet. Handle the pups gentle and firmly, to get them used to having all parts of their bodies examined: ears, teeth, coat, paws and underbelly. Give them their first worming medicine at 3 weeks, and a second dose at 5 weeks.

To cater for the bitch's needs in lactation, feed her about treble quantities in the first week, gradually decreasing, as she feeds the puppies less often (about the fifth week). She should be fed to appetite at least three times a day, and should have a good quality diet with added vitamins and minerals as devised by the vet.

The puppies should accept their first solid food at 3 weeks, and their demands on the bitch will begin to lessen about the fifth week. At 4–5 weeks they will eat as many as five meals a day. Weaning should be complete by 5–6 weeks.

6 weeks old By 6 weeks they are walking firmly, playing and defecating without stimulation. The baby teeth are firmly established and they use them in mock fighting and to exercise their jaws on a large marrow bone if one is provided.

You should now take considerable pains to keep harmful things out of the puppies' way: chemicals, flexes, house-plants (some kinds are poisonous to dogs), objects of a swallowable size. Drinking water should be offered, and eventually the puppies will learn that it is for drinking and not for paddling.

The weanling puppy

The period in a puppy's life between weaning and settling into its new home can be critical. It is a period of rapid development, both physical and mental.

Puppies are usually sold at about 8 weeks of age and it is important that the fortnightly doses of worming medicine given at 3 and 5 weeks are continued at 7, 9, 11 and 13 weeks to eliminate any chance of the puppy presenting a danger to children by harbouring roundworm. Thereafter the puppy must be wormed at 6-month intervals.

The period of 'socialization' is the period from before weaning to about 14 weeks. It is during this time that the

How to give a worming dose

*Golden Retriever puppies soon after weaning –
learning to negotiate*

young dog learns to respond socially and to recognize
its own species. One of the things that helped the dog to
become a domestic animal in the first place was its
ability, during the socialization period, to accept other
creatures, notably man.

Ideally, puppies should be taken from their mother
and siblings at about 8–10 weeks, having enjoyed the
first part of the period of socialization with dogs, while
having the remainder in which to explore and develop
lasting relationships with humans.

Breed history

The spread and improvement of retrievers in Britain was in part a response to the 19th-century fashion for wildfowling, which grew up with the arrival on the market of cheaply manufactured sporting weapons. The industrial revolution made it possible to produce firearms at prices within the means of professional gentlemen all over the country.

Wildfowling was the ideal gentleman's sport, providing country exercise in the style of the nobility and some tangible rewards to bring home for the family table. The sportsmen would journey to the moors for upland shooting, or to the marshes for gamebirds and winter visiting wildfowl.

They needed gundogs that were hardy enough to take to marsh or water in the extreme cold, which guaranteed a profitable business to gundog breeders who could acquire a good strain of really weather-resistant dogs such as the Labrador.

Our first knowledge of a dog matching the description of a modern retriever is from the 1820s, in Newfoundland, where it appears to have been called the Newfoundland Retriever. The two forms of this breed worked there as wildfowlers' dogs and, in the period before the sport was so widespread, they apparently

On a winter shoot

A Newfoundland Retriever: the Labrador began as a variant of this breed

worked in the fishing industry, helping fishermen by catching cod that had slipped the nets.

How did the dogs come to be in Newfoundland in the first place? All we know is that the coast of Newfoundland was settled in the 16th century by fishermen from Devon, and that they took dogs from England when they went there.

The Labrador Retriever

Newfoundland is the easternmost province of Canada today, consisting of **Newfoundland Island** (with the capital, St John's) and **Labrador** on the mainland next to Quebec. Its climate is harsher than that of the British Isles, and any working dogs in its wilderness of lakes, rivers and mountains had to be capable of taking tough conditions in their stride.

In 1822 a traveller to Newfoundland wrote:

'The dogs are admirably trained as retrievers in fowling, and are otherwise useful . . . The smooth or short-haired dog is preferred because in frosty weather the long-haired kind become encumbered with ice on coming out of the water.'

In 1930 another traveller, the British sportsman Colonel Hawker, described these two breeds: the 'ordinary' Newfoundland Retriever was 'very large, strong of limb, rough hair, and carrying his tail high'; and the St John's breed was:

> 'by far the best for any kind of shooting. He is generally black and no bigger than a Pointer, very fine in legs, with short hair, and does not carry his tail so much curled as the other; is extremely quick, running, swimming, fighting . . . and their sense of smell is hardly to be credited . . .'

It is believed that this St John's Newfoundland is the one the Earl of Malmesbury chose when, in 1835, he imported dogs from Newfoundland to Britain. He or his grandson later gave this strain the name of Labradors. The earliest written evidence of this name is a letter his grandson (a later Earl of Malmesbury) wrote in 1887, in which he stated:

> 'We always call mine Labrador dogs, and I have kept the breed as pure as I could from the first I (sic) had them from Poole, at that time carrying on a brisk trade with Newfoundland. The real breed may be known by its close coat which turns the water off like oil, and, above all, a tail like an otter.'

The next phase of the history of the Labrador took place in Britain. Westminster imposed a heavy tax on dogs in Newfoundland, which drove the local breed into obscurity. Quarantine laws virtually stopped the importation of fresh stock into Britain. Descendants of the original dogs are still to be seen in Newfoundland but the British breed has been given a different type, taller in the forequarters and more elastic in the gait.

In the early years of the British breed there was some crossing with other retrievers, possibly just to keep the breed going. One product of this interbreeding was the Flat-coated Retriever, a breed which for some decades was more popular then the Labrador.

Fortunately the salient characteristics of the Labrador were preserved, and a standard was drawn up in 1916 to discourage any further interbreeding. The Kennel Club granted recognition to the Labrador Retriever in 1903 and since then the breed has held its own, both at shows and field trials.

Labradors began to be exported to countries all round the world. During the 1920s and early 1930s they began to be seen in appreciable numbers in America, and the first gundog trial in America at which there were Labrador Retrievers was held in 1931 in New York state, with 16 Labradors in the Open-all-ages class.

Since its first appearance in field trial awards in the UK in 1904 the Labrador has become acknowledged as the retriever 'par excellence', dominating the scene both at field trials and as a family shooting dog.

At first almost all Labradors were black, but the Yellows have become the most popular colour now. There are also Chocolate Labradors today, though they are less common in the UK.

The Golden Retriever

As the St John's Retriever began to spread round the country estates of England and Scotland, several owners attempted to develop the breed further. One line of breeding activity led to the Flat-coated Retriever and thence, with the work of Lord Tweedmouth in Scotland, to the Golden Retriever.

Tweedmouth's estate was at Guisachan on the River Tweed, near Inverness. The country alongside this river was the home of a breed known as the Tweed Water Spaniel, which looked like a small English Retriever but had a light curl in its coat with only slight feathering (the Tweed and the English Retriever are both extinct breeds today).

Tweedmouth had a so-called Flat-coated Retriever, a male called Nous (Greek for 'wisdom') whose coat was actually beautifully wavy, and a splendid golden hue. He had bought Nous from the Earl of Chichester in 1865 because of his interest in the dog's coat.

Nous was mated to a Tweed Water Spaniel, producing four yellow puppies. This generation was crossed with Water Spaniels again, producing more yellow puppies. Further cross-breeding, using an Irish Setter and possibly a Bloodhound, developed a strain with a magnificent gold-coloured coat.

Tweedmouth was not the only breeder to be working in this direction but he was the foremost in the field and in the early years of the 20th century he fixed the type and colour of his stock so that it bred true. In 1913 the Kennel Club recognized it as a separate breed, distinct from the Flat-coat at last. The Golden Retriever Club was established in the same year.

The Golden Retriever gained in popularity, not only because of the continuing fashion for wildfowling but for its generally appealing temperament and looks. It is highly intelligent and will make a good guide dog for the blind; and its obedient nature makes it much sought after for showing, while it always gets on well with children and is an excellent family dog.

The Golden Retriever has been found the most successful breed for a new venture in care for the disabled. After pioneer work for some years in America and the Netherlands, a new organization, 'Guide Dogs for the Disabled' is to be set up in Britain. Golden Retrievers are also conspicuous helpers in the PAT scheme for visiting the sick in hospitals.

The Golden Retriever has been exported to the USA and Canada since the 1890s, and is today popular in Australia and Western Europe, particularly Scandinavia as well. In 1986 and 1987 the Golden Retriever Club organized exchange visits with the Golden Retriever Club of Denmark; and links with the Belgian club were also being promoted with similar visits in 1987. The club has also been in recent years to the Netherlands and Switzerland, and the system of annual visits to clubs overseas is well established and is being developed with vigour for the future.

Index

Figures in italics refer to illustrations